Hillary Rodham Clinton

Hillary Rodham Clinton

★★★★★★★★★★★★★★★★★★★★★★

1947–

BY DEBORAH KENT

CHILDREN'S PRESS®
A Division of Grolier Publishing
New York   London   Hong Kong   Sydney
Danbury, Connecticut

Consultants: ALAN SCHECHTER
                 Professor
                 Vice Chairman, J. William Fulbright Foreign Scholarship Board
                 Department of Political Science
                 Wellesley College, Wellesley, Massachusetts
                 LINDA CORNWELL
                 Learning Resource Consultant
                 Indiana Department of Education

Project Editor: DOWNING PUBLISHING SERVICES
Page Layout: CAROLE DESNOES
Photo Researcher: JAN IZZO

Visit Children's Press on the Internet at:
http://publishing.grolier.com

Library of Congress Cataloging-in-Publication Data
Kent, Deborah
        Hillary Rodham Clinton: 1947– / by Deborah Kent
             p.   cm. — (Encyclopedia of first ladies)
        Includes bibliographical references and index.
        Summary: A biography of the wife of the forty-second president of the United States,
discussing her youth, marriage, and work on health care and the welfare and education of
children.
        ISBN 0-516-20644-3
        1. Clinton, Hillary Rodham—Juvenile literature. 2. Presidents' spouses—United
States—Biography—Juvenile literature. [1. Clinton, Hillary Rodham.   2. First ladies.
3. Women—Biography.]
E887.C55K46   1998
973.929'092—dc21   97–48243
[B]   CIP
                                                      AC

Table of Contents

Hillary Rodham Clinton

CHAPTER ONE

The Girl Who Could Play with the Boys

* * * * * * * * * * * * * * * * * *

One day when Hillary Rodham was four years old, she rushed to her mother in tears. She had run into trouble with the local bully, a little girl who lived up the street. The bully had hit her. She wouldn't let Hillary play with the other neighborhood children, most of whom were boys. When Hillary stopped crying, her mother told her to go back outside. If the bully bothered her again, Hillary should hit her back.

The next time she met the bully, Hillary chased her away. Then she ran home and announced joyfully, "I can play with the boys now!"

Dorothy Rodham, Hillary's mother, was determined

* * * * * * * * * * * * * * * * * *

that her daughter should never feel limited simply because she was a girl. She encouraged Hillary to play baseball, to stand up for herself in a fight, and always to speak her mind. She chose the name Hillary for her daughter because it was unusual. At that time, it was a name most often given to boys.

Hillary Diane Rodham was born in Chicago on October 26, 1947. In 1950, her family moved to a two-story brick house in a nearby suburb called Park Ridge. Park Ridge was an ideal place for children. The streets were safe, the neighbors were friendly, and the schools were outstanding. Dozens of other children lived within a few blocks of the Rodhams' house. Hillary and her two younger brothers always carried the first-ever World Series television broadcast: the New York Yankees beat the Brooklyn Dodgers four games to three. Jackie Robinson, the first African-American player admitted to the major leagues, played for Brooklyn. He was made 1947's Rookie of the Year but was repeatedly refused hotel rooms because of his skin color.

Teenagers, no longer living in the gloom of war, could finally enjoy their youth. Bobbysoxers gathered around jukeboxes to swoon over the music of young Frank Sinatra. Drive-in movies and soda fountains swarmed with legions of blue-jeaned teens escaping the watchful eye of parents. Bubble-gum-blowing contests took the country by storm.

Into the good times, however, crept a new phrase: *cold war.* The Cold War, a political and military standoff between the two world superpowers, the United States and communist Russia, settled in like a deep freeze. In spite of their prosperity and optimism, Americans lived in its chilly shadow, fearing Russian expansion in Europe, the spread of communism, and the threat of nuclear war. People like Hillary, born in 1947 or after, grew up with the Cold War and rejoiced when its spell was finally broken in 1991 with the breakup of the Soviet Union.

In 1950, the Rodhams moved into this two-story brick house in suburban Park Ridge, Illinois.

Pickwick Theater in downtown Park Ridge, Illinois

had plenty of friends. They ran from yard to yard playing tag, cops and robbers, and hide-and-seek. The grown-ups sat on their porches, talking and watching everything that went on.

Hugh Rodham, Hillary's father, was proud to be raising his children in such a lovely setting. His own childhood had not been an easy one. He grew up in Scranton, Pennsylvania, the son of immigrants from England. His father worked in a textile factory. Hugh Rodham was also in the textile business. He ran a small company that

A view of Prospect Avenue, downtown Park Ridge

Hillary Rodham's sixth-grade class picture, Field School, 1959. Hillary is in the first row, far right.

Illinois, U.S.A.

✷ ✷

Chicago, the city where Hillary Rodham was born in 1947, is located in the north-eastern corner of Illinois on the shores of Lake Michigan. Although it is not the capital of the state, it is by far the state's largest city. In 1947, it was second only to New York City in its population. Chicago is perhaps most famous for the fire that destroyed the heart of the city in 1871 and for its wild days in the 1920s and 1930s as a haven for gangsters such as Al Capone. Capone died in 1947, however, and the city's reputation for crime was already being replaced by its reputation for deep-dish pizza. During Hillary's childhood in Park Ridge, neighboring O'Hare Airport, soon the world's busiest, began operations, and the first McDonald's restaurant opened in nearby Des Plaines.

Beyond the hustle and bustle of the Chicagoland area, nearly 80 percent of Illinois' 56,400 square miles (146,076 square kilometers) is quiet farmland. The mighty Mississippi River forms the state's western boundary. Springfield, Illinois, the capital since 1839, is located toward the middle of the state and is perhaps best known as the home of sixteenth president Abraham Lincoln.

Hillary Rodham (standing, second from left) was a member of her high-school debate club.

Hillary (middle row, second from right) was also a member of the National Honor Society.

Hillary (front, center) as a member of the student council in her Park Ridge high school

sold draperies. He might have been a factory worker himself if he had not won a football scholarship to Pennsylvania State University. Education, he believed, was the route out of poverty. He often said he believed in "learning for earning's sake."

Hillary loved school. She worked hard and received excellent grades. But her father urged her to try even harder. Sometimes when her report card showed straight A's he remarked, "That must be an easy school you go to." Hillary took his comment as a challenge, and tried to do better still.

Virtually all of the families in Park Ridge were white and prosperous.

Hillary (front) was a National Merit finalist.

Hillary Rodham attended Maine Township High School South in Park Ridge.

Hillary and her friends took their privileged existence for granted. They knew almost nothing about life beyond their comfortable suburb. Then, when Hillary was fourteen, a new youth director came to the Methodist church her family attended. The Reverend Don Jones believed that young people should become involved in social and political causes. His views exposed Hillary to a more complex view of the world.

Don Jones felt that Christians should not be concerned merely with their personal salvation. They should work to help others, to make the world a better place. He encouraged the teens in his youth group to babysit for the children of migrant farmworkers in the nearby town of Des Plaines. He organized joint programs with youth groups from Chicago's tough inner-city neighborhoods. Often, he used music and art to open up discussions among young people from vastly different backgrounds.

Hillary and her family attended the First United Methodist Church of Park Ridge, where the Reverend Don Jones was youth director.

Jones once brought a copy of Pablo Picasso's famous painting *Guernica* to a youth meeting. The painting depicts the horrors of war in a tumultuous battle scene. Jones had the teens look at the painting in silence for several minutes. Then he asked them to describe the feelings it awakened. The inner-city teens had much more to say than those from Park Ridge. One girl broke into sobs and explained that her uncle had been shot three days before when he took a neighbor's parking place. "Why?" she cried. "Why did he have to die?"

In 1962, Rev. Jones took the youth group to hear a speech by Dr. Martin Luther King Jr. Dr. King, the revered leader of the civil-rights movement for African-Americans, spoke to 2,500

To stimulate discussion among teens from Park Ridge and the inner city, Rev. Don Jones once brought a copy of this Pablo Picasso painting, Guernica, to a youth group meeting.

Dr. Martin Luther King Jr.

people at Orchestra Hall in Chicago. Hillary was thrilled by his call to action. Afterward, Rev. Jones led the students backstage to meet Dr. King in person. Hillary never forgot the moment when she shook Dr. King's hand.

Like most people in Park Ridge, Hillary Rodham's parents were staunch Republicans. During the presidential election of 1964, they supported the conservative Republican candidate, Barry Goldwater. Hillary,

Worlds Apart

✮ ✮

It's no wonder the thoughtful Hillary felt confused during the 1964 presidential election. Democrats and Republicans had very different ideas about the issues. Candidate Lyndon Johnson represented the Democratic party's philosophy of using the federal government and its money as a tool to improve the lives of U.S. citizens. Republican candidate Barry Goldwater and his conservative supporters believed that government should stay out of people's lives and serve only the basic needs of defense and keeping order. Conservatives were greatly concerned with the national debt and wanted Congress to okay only those programs the government could pay for up-front, thereby balancing the federal budget. Democrats felt that such deep cuts in government spending would leave too many poor people without needed aid. Democrats and Republicans also held very different views on foreign affairs. Whereas Democrats were willing to negotiate with the Communist government of the Soviet Union and hoped to stop nuclear weapons tests, Republicans' deep distrust of the Soviets led them to believe the United States should not give an inch in the arms race. Looking upward, too, the parties had differing priorities. Democrats wanted to plunge the United States into the age of space exploration. Republicans advocated reorganizing the space program in order to spend less on NASA. Who won the 1964 election? Lyndon Johnson, in a huge landslide.

too, became an ardent Goldwater supporter. Yet at the same time, she continued to absorb Rev. Jones's liberal ideas. She was discovering that the world was far more complicated than she had ever imagined.

During Hillary's senior year in high school, she and her friends talked endlessly about the future. Many of the girls planned to attend local colleges. They did not expect to have careers beyond marriage and

Ms. America

✮ ✮

Young Hillary found herself in the middle of an exciting and confusing time for American women. In 1964, Congress passed the Civil Rights Act, which made it illegal to discriminate in the workplace on the basis of color or gender. Perhaps the time had finally come for women to realize the equality they had dreamed of for over a hundred years.

In the late 1960s, the struggle for women's rights became known as the "women's liberation movement," or just "women's lib," but it had been going on for a long time. Back in 1848, a group of women had come together to demand equality with men in all respects. In those days, women's rights were extremely limited. Married women couldn't even own property, and no female could speak in public. And they certainly couldn't vote. Not until seventy-two years later, in 1920, did women win that right.

Although many battles had been won by the 1960s, women still faced fewer employment opportunities and lesser pay than men. True, in 1960, more women were working outside the home than ever before, but they began to feel frustrated by their limited choices. Many women felt forced by society into the traditional female roles of mother and housekeeper at home and teacher and nurse in the workplace. There was little demand for female lawyers, doctors, engineers, or architects, and college-educated women earned only half what men with the same training earned. Inspired by the civil-rights movement to end discrimination against African-Americans, women took up their own cause of equality. The 1960s echoed with strong and often angry words, protests, and demonstrations as women attempted to be heard.

While the story of women's rights is far from over, women today benefit from the groundwork laid by the feminists of the 1960s and more than a century of women before them.

In 1964, Republican presidential candidate Barry Goldwater (left) campaigned with Charles Percy, candidate for governor of Illinois.

motherhood. Hillary wanted something more. She loved to study, and political issues were her passion. Her friends joked that someday she would be the first female president of the United States.

One of Hillary's high-school teachers was a graduate of Wellesley College, a prestigious women's college near Boston, Massachusetts. With her teacher's encouragement, Hillary applied to Wellesley and was accepted. In the fall of 1965, she set out from home on her first great adventure.

☆ ☆ ☆ ☆ ☆ ☆ ☆ ☆ ☆ ☆ ☆ ☆ ☆ ☆ ☆

CHAPTER TWO

Student Dreams

* * * * * * * * * * * * * * * * * *

During her freshman year at Wellesley, Hillary Rodham often wrote to her old friend and mentor, the Reverend Don Jones. She told him that college gave her the chance to explore many new identities. That January, she tried to study during every spare minute. "After six weeks of little human communication or companionship, my diet of reading and writing gave me indigestion," she wrote. "The last two weeks of February here were an orgy of decadent indulgence, as decadent as any upright Methodist can become." In March, Hillary became a social reformer. By April, she had painted a flower on her arm in hippie style.

* * * * * * * * * * * * * * * * *

Flower Power

✳ ✳

Across the country, Hillary's generation questioned the authority of their institutions, parents, and government. They came to be known as hippies and flower children, and the most extreme among them rejected "establishment" values in favor of a lifestyle as different from their parents as possible. Jeans, beads, and tie-dyed T-shirts became their uniform, rock music their soundtrack, and flowers their symbol of peace and love. Men and women wore their hair long or, among African-Americans, in the curly Afro style. Terms such as *groovy, right on,* and *far out* replaced the old-fashioned *cool, swell,* and *neat.* At love-ins, be-ins, and happenings of all sizes, hippies gathered to commune with one another, dance, listen to music, and, sometimes, smoke marijuana. In San Francisco's Golden Gate Park in January 1967, and again in New York's Central Park that spring, more than 10,000 young people dressed in exotic costumes and decorated with face and body paint gathered for a day of music, dancing, and celebrating. A triumph of the hippie culture, the famous concert at Woodstock in 1969 offered three days of live outdoor music—much of it in the rain—to an incredibly peaceful crowd of half a million people.

College offered Hillary a wonderful opportunity for learning—about history, about literature, about world affairs, and about herself.

Hillary was a tall, slender girl who wore glasses. She seldom used make-up. Her straight blonde hair hung loosely to her shoulders. She could seem cold and aloof to strangers, too quick to criticize and pass judgment. Those who knew her well, however, found her to be a warm and loyal friend.

Like most of her classmates, Hillary enjoyed going to dances and parties. She could be silly and giggly at times. But most of all she loved to talk seriously about ideas. Night after

Hillary Rodham
attended Wellesley
College in Wellesley,
Massachusetts.

A candid shot of
Hillary taken for the
1969 Wellesley
College yearbook

Vietnam War: Fast Facts

WHAT: Conflict over control of the Southeast Asian nation of Vietnam

WHEN: 1957–1975

WHO: The United States, South Vietnam, and various allies opposed the North Vietnamese and the Viet Cong

WHERE: Throughout North and South Vietnam, and later into Cambodia and Laos

WHY: In the early 1950s, the French controlled Vietnam. Fearing a Communist takeover of Vietnam and the rest of Southeast Asia, American leaders supported the French. When the French withdrew, the United States sent military advisers to help train the South Vietnamese to oppose the Communist north. America became more and more involved until U.S. troops were actually fighting alongside the South Vietnamese in a war against North Vietnam.

OUTCOME: Direct American military involvement ended with a cease-fire in 1973. In all, 58,000 American soldiers and about 1 million North and South Vietnamese perished. In 1975, the North invaded the South, and the capital of Saigon surrendered. Today, a unified Vietnam lives under Communist rule.

Hillary Rodham was one of many college students who believed the United States should not have become involved in the Vietnam War.

night, she and her friends stayed up late discussing philosophy and politics. They felt that they should use their talents, education, and energy to solve the world's problems. "We arrived not knowing what was not possible," Hillary stated years later in an interview. "Consequently, we expected a lot."

One of the most compelling issues for Hillary and her classmates was the war that raged in Vietnam. Hillary deplored the destruction and blood-

shed. More and more, she questioned why the United States had become involved in the conflict. Gradually, she came to believe that her country was making a dreadful mistake by fighting in this faraway land.

On April 4, 1968, Hillary heard the terrible news that Dr. Martin Luther King Jr. had just been assassinated. Later her roommate remembered, "Suddenly the door flew open. Her bookbag flew across the room and slammed into the wall. She was dis-

Martin Luther King Jr. (1929–1968)

✫ ✫

This brilliant and well-spoken Baptist minister became America's leading advocate for civil rights through nonviolence in the 1960s. Born in Atlanta as Michael Luther King, his preacher father later changed both their names to honor the great Protestant reformer Martin Luther. At age fifteen, Martin entered Morehouse College and by eighteen was ordained in his father's church. He continued his education, earning his Ph.D. from Boston University in 1955. A born leader and inspiring speaker, Dr. King rose to prominence urging his followers to practice "passive resistance," or nonviolence, in their quest for civil rights. In doing so, he gave African-Americans a powerful new weapon against hate, discrimination, and prejudice. In his most famous speech, delivered in 1963 in a massive march on Washington, Dr. King described his dream that "one day we will live in a nation where [my children] will not be judged by the color of their skin but by the content of their character." Sadly, even the eloquent Dr. King could not hold back the tide of violence that would erupt in the ongoing struggle for civil rights. He himself fell victim to an assassin's bullet on April 4, 1968.

traught. She was yelling. She kept asking questions. She said, 'I can't stand it any more! I can't take it!' She was crying." Hillary and some of her friends put on black armbands and went into Boston. They joined thousands of people who poured into the streets to mourn together, tormented by anger and pain.

That summer, after completing her junior year at Wellesley, Hillary went to Washington as an intern with the House Republican Conference. There, in the nation's capital, she observed the political process in action. Toward the end of the summer, she attended the Republican National Convention in Miami. Then, late in August, she went home to visit her family in Park Ridge. The Democratic

Crowds gathered in Atlanta on April 9, 1968, the day of Martin Luther King Jr.'s funeral at Ebenezer Baptist Church.

Hillary joined this crowd of students who gathered on Boston Common to mourn the death of Dr. Martin Luther King Jr.

29

Chicago, 1968

✮ ✮

Richard Nixon was elected to the presidency in 1968 against a backdrop of disorder and unrest. The Democrats nominated Vice President Hubert Humphrey to be their candidate. His nomination had been marred by violence. Nearly 10,000 young people gathered in Chicago during the convention in August of 1968 to protest the war in Vietnam. Some were angry and violent; others came hoping simply to be heard. Nearly 20,000 law-enforcement officers stood by to keep the peace. But riots erupted in the streets and parks, even as convention delegates across town nominated their man. Afterward, candidate Nixon pointed to the disturbing events at the Democratic convention, promising to heal the nation's wounds. His pledge soothed ordinary Americans upset by the week of violence in Chicago, and they made him the next president.

An antiwar demonstration in Chicago

National Convention was being held in Chicago. Hillary and a few of her friends went into the city to see what was going on. They were shocked when members of the Chicago police force attacked a group of antiwar demonstrators in the city's Grant Park. As Hillary watched, police officers beat the unarmed protesters with clubs and threw them into paddy wag-

31

Hillary Rodham (center) was elected president of Wellesley College Student Government.

ons. How could such a thing happen, she wondered, in a country that guaranteed the right to freedom of speech? In a country that claimed to protect its citizens from needless violence?

When Hillary returned to Wellesley that fall, she had the chance to view politics from a different angle. She had been elected to serve as president of the student government. She used her position to encourage more student participation in decision-making about campus life. At the same time, she wrote a thesis on the efforts of the federal government to improve the lives of the poor.

As commencement approached, many of the seniors wanted a student to speak at the ceremony. At first, the college administration said no. Commencement speakers were always members of the faculty or prominent outsiders. That year, the college had invited Massachusetts Senator Edward Brooke to speak. But the students persisted, and at last they won their case. A student speaker would be added to the commencement program. The students chose Hillary Rodham to speak for them on commencement day.

In the weeks before graduation, Hillary gathered ideas from her classmates. She wanted to capture their concerns as they prepared to enter the "real world." Before the ceremony, she wrote out her speech and showed it to several college officials. Her comments met with their complete approval.

Hillary was scheduled to speak immediately after Senator Brooke gave his address. The senator's speech was bland and noncommittal. It skirted carefully around the war and other controversial topics. To Hillary, it symbolized much that was wrong with the United States. When she rose to speak, she put aside her notes and began spontaneously, "Senator Brooke's remarks reflected just the kind of disconnected, irrelevant thinking that has led the country astray for four years." She went on to explain why she and so many other students wanted something more from public officials. She concluded, "We are all of us exploring a world that none of us understand, and attempting to create within that uncertainty. We're searching for more immediate, ecstatic, and penetrating modes of living."

Some college officials and parents were appalled, but the students and many faculty members clapped and

Hillary Rodham gave the student speech at the Wellesley College commencement program.

cheered. Reporters snapped photos. Excerpts from Hillary's speech appeared in *Life* magazine. For a little while, Hillary Rodham was a national celebrity. She seemed to be the voice for a young generation that challenged the way things were and dreamed of a world that someday could be.

CHAPTER THREE

The Young Man from Arkansas

☆ ☆ ☆ ☆ ☆ ☆ ☆ ☆ ☆ ☆ ☆ ☆ ☆ ☆ ☆

In the fall of 1969, Hillary Rodham entered Yale University School of Law in New Haven, Connecticut. Yale has one of the finest law schools in the country. It demands a great deal from its students. Anyone who completes the program can look forward to a promising career.

One day during her second year at Yale, Hillary noticed a handsome young man talking to a group of other students. As she passed, she overheard him exclaim, "And we grow the biggest watermelons in the world!" "Who is that?" Hillary asked a friend. "Oh," her friend replied, "that's Bill Clinton. He's from

☆ ☆ ☆ ☆ ☆ ☆ ☆ ☆ ☆ ☆ ☆ ☆ ☆ ☆ ☆

Yale University Law School

Arkansas. That's all he ever talks about."

A few weeks later, Hillary sat in the law school library. Looking up from her book, she saw Bill Clinton watching her. She returned to her reading. When she glanced up again,

Bill was still there. He hadn't taken his eyes from her.

Hillary pushed back her chair and walked toward him. "Look," she said, "you've been staring at me for five minutes. The least you can do is introduce yourself." Clinton was so startled

Life at Law School

★ ★

It is not at all unusual that two law students would meet for the first time in the library. Students in law school spend the majority of their time reading and studying. No matter where your interest lies, as Hillary's did in laws affecting children, all types of law have to be mastered, such as tax, real estate, and property law. Students also study the rules of courtroom procedure for both civil and criminal trials. Competition is fierce to get the best grades and to be accepted to write for the school's best journals. Students are often very political, and life at law school often mirrors current events and controversies. Because law students work so hard to graduate, it is amazing that they have any time for a social life at all!

Sterling Law Quadrangle, Yale University

Virginia Dwire-Kelly, Bill Clinton's mother

the same time," she said years later. "I just never had met anybody like that. It was a unique combination, particularly at a place like Yale Law School, where stresses and ambitions are all very focused. Bill was extraordinary in his interest in other people."

William Jefferson Clinton was born in Hope, Arkansas, in 1946. A few months before his birth, his father was killed in an automobile accident. Bill's mother later married again. Her second husband, Bill's stepfather, was an alcoholic. Clinton's childhood was marred by family strife.

On the surface, Bill Clinton and Hillary Rodham seemed to have little in common. Bill's family struggled with emotional and financial problems; Hillary grew up in an affluent home with loving, supportive parents. Arkansas, where Bill Clinton came from, was one of the poorest, least-developed states in the nation. Hillary came from an upper-middle-class suburb of Chicago, one of the country's leading cities.

Despite their differences, however, Bill and Hillary were remarkably similar. Like Hillary, Bill was a brilliant

he could barely speak. But he stammered out his name, and the two began to talk.

From the beginning, Hillary was drawn by Bill Clinton's warmth and charm. "I was struck by how he was able to be so smart and so human at

Mines and Minds

✷ ✷ ✷ ✷ ✷ ✷ ✷ ✷ ✷ ✷ ✷ ✷ ✷ ✷ ✷ ✷ ✷ ✷ ✷

The prestigious Rhodes Scholarship is named for Cecil John Rhodes. Born into a middle-class English family, Cecil Rhodes left for Africa to shape his fortune in 1870 and ended up shaping the history of South Africa and the world's diamond industry. When he wasn't mining diamonds, he earned his bachelor's degree from Oxford University. The founder of Rhodesia, now Zambia and Zimbabwe, Rhodes dreamed of establishing an elite group of talented, dedicated, and wealthy men to administer the govern-

Cecil Rhodes

ments of the world. In his will, he created the financial backing for the Rhodes Scholarship program. Under the program, men (and women, after 1976) from the United States and seventeen other countries were allowed to study for two years at Oxford University. Today, the scholarship is based on success in leadership, academics, and sports. As a Rhodes Scholar, Bill Clinton is in good company with Supreme Court Justice Byron White; the first poet laureate of the United States, Robert Penn Warren; and Senator William Fulbright, who worked to create an American program for the international exchange of scholars.

Supreme Court Justice
Byron White

Poet Laureate Robert
Penn Warrren

Senator William
Fulbright

President Clinton received an honorary degree from Oxford University in 1994, twenty-four years after he had attended Oxford on a Rhodes Scholarship.

student. He had even spent two years studying at Oxford University in England as the winner of a coveted Rhodes Scholarship. Furthermore, both Bill and Hillary shared a deep commitment to social justice. They were fiercely ambitious, and they wanted to build a better world for everyone.

As time passed, Hillary and Bill grew closer and closer. "It's hard to describe the chemistry," recalled one of Bill's roommates. "Hillary had a sharp mind coupled with a traditional midwestern openness. Bill was the quintessential southerner, charming and gregarious. It was fun to watch the dance."

A few months after Hillary met Clinton, she went to a lecture given by Marian Wright Edelman. Edelman was the first African-American woman ever licensed to practice law in Mississippi. As Edelman talked

Marian Wright Edelman, an African-American lawyer who is deeply concerned with the plight of children in the United States, is shown here at a Celebration of Children in Washington, D.C.

41

Marian Wright Edelman (1939–)

✮ ✮

Hillary could have wished for no better inspiration in her work with children than Marian Wright Edelman. Marian, the youngest of five children, was born to a Baptist minister in Bennettsville, South Carolina, on June 6, 1939. Her mother and father lived their preaching by starting and running a home for the elderly, teaching Marian early to feel responsible for others. After entering Spelman College in Atlanta, Marian's academic excellence won her the chance

to spend the next year abroad studying in Paris, Switzerland, and the Soviet Union. She returned after a year to racial upheaval in the South and threw herself into the civil-rights movement. After law school, she became a civil-rights lawyer and eventually the first African-American woman to pass the bar exam in Mississippi. In 1973, she founded the Children's Defense Fund, one of the country's most effective organizations at keeping the problems and needs of children in the public eye. The fund encourages government and private action to help children *before* sickness, need, family collapse, abuse, or other problems ruin their chances for a good life.

Marian Wright Edelman

about her experiences in the civil-rights movement, Hillary was enthralled. After the lecture, she told Edelman that she would like to work for her someday. Edelman invited Hillary to work that summer on a project researching the conditions among migrant farmworkers. Hillary leaped at the chance.

Marian Wright Edelman was deeply concerned with the plight of children in the United States. Hillary realized that she, too, wanted children to be the focus of her professional life. She determined to use the law to protect children from mistreatment and neglect. After graduating from Yale, she spent another year in New Haven working with the Yale Child Study Center. She researched the way the legal system handled child abuse, foster care, and other issues affecting children's lives.

Bill Clinton, too, knew what he wanted to do after graduation. He would return to Arkansas and run for office. By gaining power within the state government, he thought he could improve conditions for the poor and underprivileged.

As her feeling for Clinton deepened into love, Hillary wondered if she could ever share her life with him. On her own, she could take a job in Washington. She could work to shape national policy on children's rights. What kind of future could she expect if she followed Bill Clinton to Arkansas?

Clinton went back to Arkansas as soon as he graduated from Yale. He taught courses on law at the University of Arkansas in Fayetteville, and prepared to run for Congress.

Bill Clinton (left) and others greet Senator Barry Goldwater (right) as he arrives for a speaking engagement at the University of Arkansas.

Hillary did not go with him. Instead, she obtained a job with a team of lawyers developing a case against President Richard M. Nixon. In 1972, burglars had broken into Democratic campaign headquarters at Washington's Watergate Hotel. Some of Nixon's supporters were implicated. As the story unfolded, it appeared that President Nixon had tried to conceal the truth. The "Watergate Scandal" led to investigations into a complex series of cover-ups and secret deals. Now, Nixon's opponents felt that he should be impeached (charged with misconduct). Hillary was part of the team of lawyers that studied earlier impeachment cases at the state and federal levels. Their final report filled thirty-six heavy black binders.

Nixon resigned on August 9, 1974, before impeachment hearings could begin. Hillary was relieved. Nixon's resignation showed her that the democratic process could work even

Faculty member Bill Clinton speaking in the moot courtroom at the University of Arkansas Law School

44

From the Grass Roots

The civil-rights movement began in the 1950s and 1960s as ordinary Americans mounted a series of nonviolent protests to bring the problems of racism and social injustice into the public eye. In 1955, before the ministers of the South formed the Southern Christian Leadership Conference (SCLC), Mrs. Rosa Parks, a black seamstress, refused to give up her seat on the bus to a white man and went to jail for her actions. The black community in Montgomery, Alabama, organized behind her and refused to ride the city buses. The boycott was led by a local Baptist preacher named Martin Luther King Jr., who had yet to gain national recognition. In 1960, before the nation's college students created the Student Nonviolent Coordinating Committee (SNCC), four young black men from North Carolina Agricultural and Technical College sat determinedly at a Woolworth's lunch counter for hours. They were protesting against a law that stated only whites could eat there. These ordinary Americans, often faced with bodily harm and insult, refused to return violence with violence. They refused as well to endure any longer the unfair treatment they faced. Their courageous actions inspired the growth of the modern American civil-rights movement.

The 1960 Woolworth's lunch counter sit-in took place in Greensboro, North Carolina.

President Richard Nixon giving his televised resignation speech on August 9, 1974

in a crisis. But now she was out of a job. What should she do?

Bill urged her to join him in Fayetteville. A teaching job was available at the law school. Why didn't she give it a try?

Clinton knew that the decision could not be an easy one for Hillary. "This is a woman whose future is limitless," he told a friend. "She could be anything she decides to be. I feel so guilty about bringing her here, because then it would be my state, my life, and my political future."

Hillary's friends warned her against moving to Arkansas. They said she would be burying herself alive. But at last she decided to go to Fayetteville. Years later, she reflected on her struggle. "Much as I would have liked to have denied it, there was something very special about Bill," she said, "and there was something very important between us."

☆ ☆ ☆ ☆ ☆ ☆ ☆ ☆ ☆ ☆ ☆ ☆ ☆ ☆ ☆

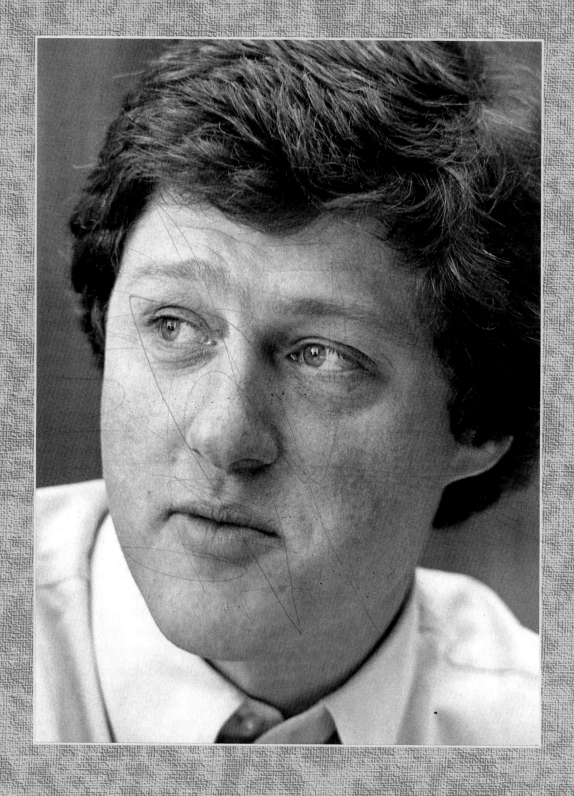

CHAPTER FOUR

"I Followed My Heart"

★ ★ ★ ★ ★ ★ ★ ★ ★ ★ ★ ★ ★ ★ ★ ★ ★

Hillary Rodham set out for Arkansas with a friend late in August 1974. Their car was piled with suitcases, boxes of books, and even a ten-speed bicycle. "It was a lollygagging, long, and aimless trip of stopping and shopping across the South," Hillary's friend explained, looking back. "She wanted to get going, but I forced her to do a little sightseeing along the way. Every twenty minutes, I told her what I thought about her burying herself in Fayetteville. 'You are crazy! You are out of your mind! You're going to this rural out-of-the-way place and you'll wind up married to some country lawyer!'"

★ ★ ★ ★ ★ ★ ★ ★ ★ ★ ★ ★ ★ ★ ★ ★ ★

Fayetteville, Arkansas, in mountain mist

Highway 74 east of Fayetteville, in the Ozark Mountains

When Hillary and her friend drove into Fayetteville, their worst nightmares seemed to be coming true. They arrived just in time for a huge University of Arkansas football rally. The sidewalks were crowded with people wearing pig hats to honor the Arkansas Razorbacks. Everywhere fans shouted, "Soo-ee! Soo-ee! Pig, pig, pig!"

Undaunted, Hillary went straight to Bill's office. By then, his congressional campaign was in full swing. Hillary stuffed envelopes, made phone calls, and organized meetings. Once, she had been a staunch Republican from Park Ridge, Illinois. Now, she was in Fayetteville, Arkansas, working tirelessly for a Democratic candidate for Congress.

The campaign gave Hillary a chance to meet hundreds of people from all across the state. For the first time, she understood why Bill loved Arkansas so deeply. "People were warm and welcoming to me," she recalled. "I felt very much at home, and it was a shock, because I had never lived in the South or in a small place. It gave me a perspective on life and helped me understand what it was like for most people." Bill Clinton lost the election, but only by a narrow margin. Both he and Hillary felt encouraged by all the support he received.

Hillary enjoyed her teaching job at the law school. Her classroom discussions were lively and stimulating. Once, when a student failed to answer a question, she pushed him almost mercilessly. At last, the young man exploded. "Why don't you leave me alone?" he demanded. "What do you expect? I just went to school in Arkansas!" Hillary was shocked. How could a student fall back on such an excuse? Why didn't he strive to do his very best, no matter how deprived he had been?

Hillary shared an apartment with her brother Hugh, who came to help with the Clinton campaign and decided to stay on. In addition to her teaching, Hillary worked several hours a week providing legal services to indigent clients. When she had spare time, she and Bill played volleyball or got together for dinner with friends. Hillary grew more and more comfort-

"Old Main" is the oldest building on the University of Arkansas campus.

able in her new surroundings. But did she really want to stay in Arkansas for the rest of her life?

The question crashed down upon her with full force when Bill Clinton asked her to marry him. "I know this is a really hard choice, because I'm committed to living in Arkansas," he told her. "Yes," Hillary replied, "it's a really hard choice."

In a torment of indecision, Hillary fled back to Park Ridge. Through long, soul-searching discussions with her family and friends, she weighed the possibilities. If she left Bill Clinton, she could take a job with a major law firm in Chicago, or help to set national policy in Washington. "But I also knew that I had to deal with a whole other side of life," she reflected later, "the emotional side, where we live and where we grow, and when all is said and done where the most important parts of life take place."

At last, Hillary reached her decision. She headed back to Fayetteville to become Bill Clinton's wife. As she explained later, "Caught between my head and my heart, I followed my heart."

Hillary and Bill wanted a small wedding service, attended only by a few close friends and relatives. Hillary's mother arrived a few days ahead of time to help with the arrangements. On the night before the ceremony, she asked to see her daughter's bridal gown. In all the excitement, Hillary had forgotten to buy one! She and her mother rushed out and found a shop that was still open. Hillary bought her wedding dress off the rack. It was a cream-colored Victorian-style gown trimmed with lace. Even without fittings and alterations, it was perfect for the occasion.

Hillary Rodham and Bill Clinton were married on October 11, 1975. Following the small private service, they gathered with some 200 friends for a gala reception. The reception was held at the home of their friend State Senator Henry Morris and his wife Anne.

After the wedding, Hillary continued to use her maiden name. At the time, such a choice was considered quite unusual. Hillary saw no reason to change her name just because she had married. She had been Hillary Rodham all her life, and Hillary Rodham she vowed to remain.

In 1976, Clinton's political career took a spectacular leap forward. He was elected to serve as the state's attorney general. At thirty, he was the youngest person in Arkansas history ever to hold that position. Clinton's election required Bill and Hillary to leave Fayetteville for Little Rock, the state capital.

Little Rock was much larger than Fayetteville, and offered Hillary more career opportunities. Within a few months, she joined the Rose Law Firm, the most powerful legal corpora-

The Little Rock, Arkansas, skyline

What's in a Name?

✶ ✶

It seemed shocking in 1975 for bride Hillary Rodham to keep her last name. In many Western cultures, it had long been traditional for a married woman to assume her husband's last name. However, that custom is by no means universal. Name changing, variations in spelling, and even special titles mean different things around the world. Names can signal passage into adulthood, marriage, special accomplishment, or age and experience. In Japan, for instance, little boys' names are followed by *-chan* until they enter school. Hispanic names routinely include both the mother's and father's last names. In Russia, last names are spelled according to their owner's gender. Nigerian children address older sisters and brothers as N'se and N'da to honor their age. In Korea, where last names come first, one part of a name indicates its owner's generation. An American Indian man might change his name several times throughout his life based on his accomplishments or failures. American Indian women never change their names. In the late 1800s, many African-Americans exchanged the last names given their ancestors by slaveholders for the names of political heroes such as George Washington. Today, many black Americans adopt African names; others, such as sports greats Muhammad Ali and Kareem Abdul-Jabbar, take names fitting their conversion to Islam.

54

The Arkansas state capitol in Little Rock

Defending the States

✮ ✮ ✮ ✮ ✮ ✮ ✮ ✮ ✮ ✮ ✮ ✮ ✮ ✮ ✮ ✮ ✮ ✮ ✮ ✮

Just as the United States attorney general heads the national Department of Justice, each state's attorney general is the chief legal officer of the state and head of the state's legal department. When necessary, this person, or employees of the state's attorney general's office, represents the people of the state in court. Although the attorney general can prosecute criminal cases, most of the time this highest legal officer of the state handles civil matters. *Civil* court cases decide matters of loss and responsibility when no law is broken. Instead of time in jail, the person found responsible, or *liable* in legal terminology, pays an amount of money determined by a jury. The state's attorney general defends the state when someone brings a complaint against the state to court. For instance, if someone fell on the icy steps of the statehouse, that person could sue the state for lost work time and medical expenses. A state's attorney general also makes complaints against people and businesses that act in ways harmful or fraudulent to residents of the state. During the Clinton presidency, the attorneys general of several states made history by suing many large cigarette-producing companies for marketing a product known to cause cancer.

Hillary speaking at the University of Arkansas during one of Bill's campaigns for governor

Bill Clinton during one of his campaigns for governor of Arkansas

Hillary watches as her husband takes the oath of office as governor of the state of Arkansas.

And Justice for All

✶ ✶ ✶ ✶ ✶ ✶ ✶ ✶ ✶ ✶ ✶ ✶ ✶

What happens if you need the help of a lawyer but are unable to afford those expensive services? In 1964, during President Johnson's administration, the Economic Opportunity Act made federal funding available to provide legal services for the poor. Funds were given to local groups to provide services to individuals and to push for legal reforms that would help the poor in various ways. Some of the cases these lawyers tried changed the requirements to receive welfare and challenged racial and

President Jimmy Carter

economic discrimination. In 1974, the programs for legal aid to the poor were transferred to a separate government agency called the Legal Services Corporation (LSC). To improve the quality of service, national support centers were established, each designed to support trial lawyers in different subject areas such as housing or bankruptcy law, or to help specific groups of people, such as the elderly or American Indians. These centers also helped gather information about the needs of the poor and the way laws affected their lives. President Carter appointed Hillary Rodham to the LSC board in 1977.

tion in the state. The job allowed her to practice family law and to take on commercial cases as well. In some of her cases, she defended giant companies that were embroiled in lawsuits. Late in 1977, President Jimmy Carter appointed her to the board of the Legal Services Corporation (LSC), a federal program to provide legal aid for poor people.

The Clintons seemed blessed by good fortune. Hillary's career was gaining momentum. Then, in 1978, Bill Clinton was elected governor of Arkansas. Hillary Rodham, attorney at law, was now Arkansas' First Lady.

CHAPTER FIVE

From the Governor's Mansion

The Governor's Mansion in Little Rock was a state-ly two-story house built in the 1940s. It over-flowed with treasures for Hillary to admire. Antique Oriental rugs graced the reception rooms. In the formal dining room hung a 200-year-old crystal chandelier from France. Guests were served from a magnificent silver punch bowl. The bowl was engraved with a map of Arkansas showing the state's many products.

Hillary had little time to enjoy the splendor of her new surroundings. She acted as the governor's hostess at state functions, but she continued to develop her law practice. In 1979, she became a partner in the

The Governor's Mansion in Little Rock is a stately two-story house with lovely furnishings.

Rose Law Firm. Never before had Arkansans had a First Lady with a career of her own.

That summer, Hillary and her husband spent a few weeks vacationing in England. Bill Clinton wanted to show Hillary the places he had grown to love during his time at Oxford. One morning, they walked together through the narrow streets of Chelsea, a picturesque section of London. They both felt carefree and happy. They had escaped the pressures of life in the Governor's Mansion, and they shared an exciting secret. Hillary was going to have a baby.

Governor Bill Clinton was a guest of Tom Brokaw on the Today Show.

Chelsea Victoria Clinton (1980–)

☆ ☆

Chelsea Clinton was born in Little Rock, Arkansas, on February 27, 1980, the last year of her father's first term as Arkansas governor. Only eleven when her dad ran for president, Chelsea lived with her grandparents in Little Rock while her parents traveled the country. In 1993, the family moved into the White House, where Secret Service agents gave her the code name "Energy." Chelsea attended the Sidwell Friends School, where she enjoyed science and history. Her favorite sports were soccer and volleyball. Both of Chelsea's parents worked at home—the White House —and the Clintons made dinner together a family rule. They often

skipped Washington society events to keep life as normal as possible for their daughter. They also worked to keep her out of the public eye, and the press respected this parental protection. Being first child does have some perks, however. For Chelsea, these included a sixteenth birthday paintball party at Camp David and traveling all over the world. Like the proud parents of any college-bound freshman, both Bill and Hillary Clinton accompanied their daughter when she entered Stanford University in the fall of 1997. She started her year there like any other student, if you don't count her arrival on *Air Force One.*

Suddenly Bill began to sing out loud. He sang a song called "Chelsea Morning" that had been popular in the late 1960s. Hillary decided that if her child was a girl, she would be named Chelsea as a remembrance of that special day.

Chelsea Victoria Clinton was born in Little Rock on February 27, 1980. By coincidence, she arrived on the birthday of William Jefferson Blythe, Bill Clinton's father, whom he never knew. Hillary stayed home from work for four months to take care of the new baby. She loved being a mother, but sometimes the challenge overwhelmed her. One night, Chelsea cried for hours. Hillary rocked her and walked her up and down until she was ready to drop from exhaustion.

Hillary and Bill at a rally in 1980 during Bill's campaign for a second term as governor

"Chelsea," she said at last, "we're in this together. You've never been a baby before, and I've never been a mother before. We're going to help each other understand all this."

When Hillary returned to work, she went to the office part-time. The Rose Law Firm let her arrange a work schedule that would still give her plenty of time with Chelsea. Hillary realized that most new parents were not so fortunate. She recognized the need for companies to give parents flexible work schedules, and to grant parental leave when a baby is born or adopted.

The governor of Arkansas serves a term of two years. In 1980, Bill Clinton campaigned for re-election. From the beginning, this campaign did not go smoothly. Many voters were unhappy with Clinton's policies.

Bill and Hillary (on the right) attended this formal dinner during his first term as governor.

Hillary Rodham Clinton, First Lady of Arkansas

Furthermore, some grumbled about Hillary's performance as First Lady. She was too tough, too masculine, too involved in her work at the law firm. Why did she insist on keeping her maiden name? How could she set a good example for the women of Arkansas?

In November 1980, Bill Clinton lost the election to his Republican opponent, Frank White. After he left office, he took a job in a friend's law firm. But he could not stop thinking about his defeat. Why had he lost the voters' confidence? What had gone wrong? How could he run a stronger campaign the next time? Clinton talked to people everywhere he went, trying to find the answers. "We'd go out and there'd be these confessionals in the supermarket aisles," Hillary said later. "People would come up to Bill and say they voted against him, but they were sorry he lost. And he'd say he understood and he was sorry for not listening to them better."

Clinton's defeat came at a time when Hillary's law practice was doing better than ever. The situation created tensions in the Clintons' marriage. In

1982, Clinton once again ran for governor. He had improved his campaign strategies, and approached the voters with a new sense of confidence. To help in her husband's bid for office, Hillary tried to change her image. She wore softer, more feminine hairstyles. She traded her glasses for contact lenses. And she decided to change her name. When she registered to vote she signed the form as "Hillary Rodham Clinton."

Bill Clinton comfortably won the election of 1982. Over the next ten years, he was re-elected again and again. At last, he could develop pro-

A 1983 photo of Bill Clinton as governor of Arkansas

grams to help the people of his beloved state.

Governor Clinton was deeply concerned about Arkansas' poor school system. He felt that living standards in the state could not improve unless Arkansas children received a better education. In 1983, he appointed Hillary to chair his new Educational Standards Committee. For four months, she toured the state. She talked and listened to children, parents, and teachers. "We expect nothing but the best from our athletes: discipline, teamwork, standards," she told the PTA in one small town. "I wish we could translate the same expectations and standards we have for athletics into the classroom. I wish we could give teachers the same support and praise for teaching children to read and write that we do those who teach them to throw a ball through a hoop."

Hillary insisted that high-school students should study art, music, science, and foreign languages. No student should graduate who could not pass a standardized test. Teachers, too, should be tested to show that

Bill Clinton at the 1984 National Governors Association meeting at the White House

Hillary Clinton in 1983 with Don Roberts, Director of the Arkansas State Department of Education

Governor Bill Clinton with his daughter, six-year-old Chelsea, at a voting booth during the Arkansas election of 1986

they were competent to serve in the classroom. Arkansas did not always welcome Hillary's reforms. But little by little, the schools began to raise their standards. One of Hillary's most cherished dreams had come true. She had helped to make the world a little bit better for the next generation of children.

As the 1988 presidential election drew near, leaders in the Democratic party suggested that Bill Clinton

With Some Help from His Friends

★ ★ ★ ★ ★ ★ ★ ★ ★ ★ ★ ★ ★ ★ ★ ★ ★ ★ ★ ★

Bill Clinton depended heavily on support from fellow "baby boomers," becoming the first of that generation to reach the presidency. Between World War II and 1964, more than 76 million American babies were born, making that generation the largest ever. However, with twenty years separating them, what could the oldest and youngest members of this group truly have in common? Perhaps they had more in common than any other generation. They grew up together with an amazing new invention called television. Through TV, they shared historic events, including the dawn of the nuclear age, the beginning of space exploration, the Vietnam War, and the assassinations of President John F. Kennedy, his brother Robert, and Martin Luther King Jr. The shared experience extended into their homes, as well. To supply the huge demand for housing by servicemen returning from World War II and starting families, houses were made quickly and cheaply by using simple and similar designs. In July 1945, the entire appliance industry agreed to set certain standard sizes for kitchen cabinets and appliances. Perhaps it was the sameness, or conformity, experienced in their childhood that inspired so many baby boomers to change things as they grew up. They are a generation known for political reform, social change, and rock 'n' roll.

should try for the nomination. After careful thought, Clinton decided not to run, although he opposed many of the policies of Ronald Reagan. He told the press that the campaign would be too stressful for his family, especially for seven-year-old Chelsea.

In the summer of 1991, Clinton's name was again mentioned for the Democratic nomination. He had become a prominent leader among Democratic state governors and headed a moderate organization called the Democratic Leadership Council. This time, the Clintons were ready. One evening, they sat in the Governor's Mansion with a group of friends, planning Bill's campaign. They all knew he

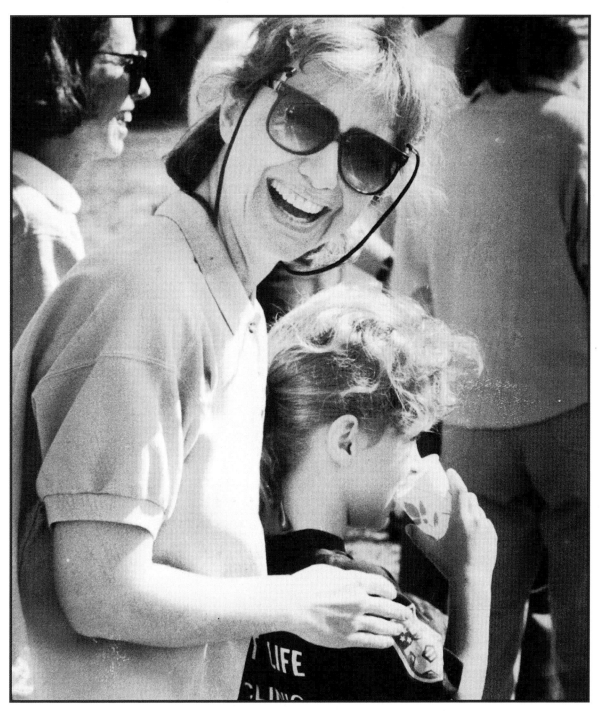

Hillary with seven-year-old Chelsea at one of Chelsea's soccer matches

George Bush (1924–)

✫ ✫

Most people remember George Bush as vice president and president between 1981 and 1993. But before he even thought about politics, George Bush played baseball for Yale, flew as a U.S. Navy bomber pilot, and started an oil company with a friend that eventually made him a millionaire. Once bitten by the political bug, he

covered even more ground. From Congress, President Nixon asked him to serve as U.S. ambassador to the United Nations, and then to run the Republican party's National Committee. President Ford sent him to China to head the country's liaison office there. (Since the United States and China had no formal relations at the time, China was not served by an American embassy.) Bush then headed the Central Intelligence Agency. Born to a well-to-do family in Massachusetts and himself a millionaire, George Bush was sometimes accused of never experiencing the hard times that less-well-off Americans face. No one could argue, though, that he hadn't worked his way up to the top.

Bill and Hillary Clinton arrive at Little Rock Airport on their return from an overseas economic trip during which the governor worked to have big businesses set up branch offices in Arkansas.

would face a difficult challenge. His opponent would be the Republican president, George Bush, who was seeking a second term. "So what happens if we win?" one friend asked. "Let's just get there first," Bill warned. But Hillary had a different answer. "We'll change things," she said.

✫ ✫ ✫ ✫ ✫ ✫ ✫ ✫ ✫ ✫ ✫ ✫ ✫ ✫ ✫

CHAPTER SIX

Into the White House

Madison Square Garden in New York City has hosted boxing matches, rock concerts, circuses, and world leaders. In 1992, it was the scene of the Democratic National Convention. Tens of thousands of people flocked to the city for the occasion. In the presidential primaries, Bill Clinton had won the largest number of delegates to the convention and therefore was the strongest candidate for the nomination. But Hillary shared the spotlight with her husband. Reporters wanted to know her opinion on everything from foreign policy to recipes for chocolate-chip cookies. She was thrilled by the crowds, the noise, and

Photos taken during Bill Clinton's 1992 primary campaign: playing the saxophone (above left) and speaking to residents (above right) at a New York City senior center; being showered with confetti at a downtown Chicago hotel (below left); and chatting at a rally in Hillary's hometown, Park Ridge, Illinois (below right)

the cameras. She was taking part in the history of her country. "I'm an old-fashioned patriot," she told one newscaster. "I cry on the Fourth of July when kids put crepe paper on their bicycle wheels. So this is just incredible! It's so extraordinary to me!"

Not all of the attention Hillary received was favorable. Again, she heard the accusation that she was unwomanly. She was too strong. She had too much to say on topics that should not concern her. She ought to keep her opinions to herself and let her husband do the talking. Bill Clinton emphasized that he and Hillary worked as a team. He valued the contribution she could make, and he hoped that the voters would, too.

When Bill Clinton won his party's nomination, the campaign began in earnest. The Clintons crossed and recrossed the United States. They talked to farmers, secretaries, factory workers, and people on unemployment lines. In 1992, the country was in a serious economic slump. Many people feared losing their jobs, their health insurance, and even their homes.

The Democratic National Convention of 1992 was held at New York City's Madison Square Garden.

The Clintons raise their arms to the crowd after Bill accepted the Democratic presidential nomination.

The Clintons join guests and delegates in a group songfest at the gala convention finale.

The Clintons (left) and the Gores (right) took a campaign bus tour through the Midwest in August.

Chelsea, Bill, and Al Gore joined Jimmy Carter at a Habitat for Humanity site in Atlanta.

If Clinton were elected, Hillary promised she would help him implement many of his programs. She would be especially involved in improving the nation's health-care system. She wanted to make health insurance available for everyone, regardless of income. "A kind of disconnect between rhetoric and action is just not going to be there," she told one audience. "If all I thought was going to happen was moving into the White House and going to Camp David for the weekends and having a ceremonial role, I think that neither Bill nor I would be there. That is just not what's at stake in this election."

Many voters were delighted when Hillary pledged to take such an active role. But others argued that she would undermine traditional family values. They claimed she regarded marriage as a form of slavery. Critics said that Hillary didn't want women to stay home and care for their husbands and children. Hillary tried to make her position clear. "You may choose to be a corporate executive or a rocket scientist," she told a group of students. "You may run for public office or you

Presidential Hideaway

☆ ☆

Created as a safe haven for President Franklin D. Roosevelt during World War II, Camp David was first known as Shangri-La and later renamed for President Eisenhower's grandson. Located on Cactotin Mountain in Maryland, the rustic resort is a short helicopter flight from the back door of the White House. Some presidents use Camp David more than others. By the time Richard Nixon became president, its cabins were sadly in need of repair. He saw that the camp was fixed up, and a good thing, too, as he escaped to Camp David during the heated days of the Watergate scandal. One of President Jimmy Carter's first orders was to get rid of the camp because he felt that the people didn't believe the president needed a posh vacation hideaway. After his staff convinced him to visit the camp, however, he fell in love with its woodsy, simple setting. It was a good thing that President Carter decided to keep the camp, since the greatest achievement of his presidency was the Middle East peace accord agreed on after days of talks at the secluded, peaceful Camp David.

may stay home and raise your children. You can now make any or all of these choices, and they can be the work of your life." Hillary was overjoyed when a group of women appeared at a rally with signs that read: "STAY-AT-HOME MOMS FOR HILLARY! WE WORK TOO!"

One of Hillary's harshest critics was former president Richard M. Nixon. "If the wife comes through as being too strong and too intelligent, it makes the husband look like a wimp," Nixon stated. Some Clinton supporters felt that Nixon carried an old grudge against Hillary. He must have remembered that she had served on the impeachment staff during the Watergate era. Hillary thought that Nixon's hostility ran still deeper.

Nothing New: Pressures of the Press

✰ ✰ ✰ ✰ ✰ ✰ ✰ ✰ ✰ ✰ ✰ ✰ ✰ ✰ ✰ ✰ ✰ ✰ ✰ ✰

Not even first president George Washington managed to avoid the pressures of the press. Just after Washington finished his farewell speech, one newspaper exclaimed that if ever a nation had suffered from improper influence, the United States certainly had under Washington. Thomas Jefferson was the first to face the "character issue" when the Richmond *Examiner* published a rumor that he had conducted a love affair with Sally Hemmings, one of his slaves. Grover Cleveland's new press secretary couldn't ward off media interest when the president married twenty-one-year-old Frances Folsom in 1886. (He was forty-nine.) Reporters and photographers lurked near the doorstep of the Clevelands' Maryland honeymoon cottage. Neither have First Ladies been spared the pressure. Few Americans can imagine the constant media attention Jacqueline Kennedy Onassis endured. Like Hillary, Eleanor Roosevelt was so harshly criticized for playing an active role in policymaking that she gave up a civil-defense job in FDR's administration and returned to a more traditional role, informally advocating the rights of immigrants, minorities, and women.

Hillary holds a baby during a campaign stop in Georgetown, Texas, on August 27, 1992.

"Maybe he knew before others knew that there was a lot going on under the surface of this country," she reflected. "People were anxious for change."

On the morning of Election Day, Bill and Hillary Clinton flew to Little Rock. The long months of campaigning were at an end. The Clintons had shared their hopes with the people of the United States. Now they could only wait to learn what the voters would decide.

Reporters and well-wishers poured into the city. Cars jammed the streets. Every hotel was full. Spectators craned to see election results that flashed across a giant outdoor television screen. At the Governor's Mansion, Hillary, Bill, and Chelsea were surrounded by dozens of friends. Even some of Hillary's former classmates from Wellesley and Park Ridge were with her on this momentous day.

By two o'clock in the afternoon, it was clear that Bill Clinton was going to win the election. The official announcement came at eleven o'clock that night. A limousine whisked the Clintons to the Old State House. There Bill Clinton gave a brief victo-

Crowds of people jammed the Old State House grounds in Little Rock on election night, 1992.

Bill and Hillary wave to the crowd after Bill declared victory on election night.

Bill with his mother the day after his election

Moving out of the Governor's Mansion

ry speech. "Today, the steelworker and the stenographer, the teacher and the nurse, had as much power in the mystery of our democracy as the president, the billionaire, and the governor," Clinton declared. "You all spoke with equal voices for change. And tomorrow we will try to give you that."

Then, Clinton turned to Chelsea and Hillary, who stood beside him on the podium. He introduced Hillary to the nation, saying, "She will be one of the greatest First Ladies in the history of the republic." The crowd broke into wild cheers and applause. A rhythmic chant swept through the hall: "Hil-la-ry! Hil-la-ry!"

In her excitement, Hillary slipped under a security rope to embrace her old friends from Park Ridge. As they hugged joyfully, Secret Service staff shouted for her to get back behind the barricade. Already, it seemed, the new First Lady was breaking the rules.

Complete with their cat, Socks, the Clintons moved into the White House in January 1993. Hillary struggled to protect her family's privacy. As much as possible, she wanted Chelsea to lead a normal life. One day, she and

First Pets

★ ★

As presidential cat, Socks joins a long list of executive pets. In the nineteenth century, John Quincy Adams raised silkworms and Andrew Johnson kept white mice. Theodore Roosevelt is famous for loving bear cubs. He had several at the executive mansion, along with a young lion. Dogs have been most popular over the years. FDR's beloved Scottie, Fala, slept on a special chair in the president's bedroom. At least two presidents had Irish setters: the Trumans called theirs Mike, and the Nixons named theirs King Timahoe. President Harding owned Laddie Boy, an airedale. Lyndon Johnson's beagles, Him and Her, were much photographed. The Ford family's golden retriever, Liberty, gave birth to nine pups in the White House. Of several Bush springer spaniels, Millie was most famous, authoring a book with her owner. To Socks's apparent dismay, a black lab puppy named Buddy moved into the Clinton White House in 1997.

Bill Clinton taking the oath of office as president on January 20, 1993

Chelsea went to a supermarket to buy groceries, like any ordinary mother and daughter. When they reached the checkout counter, the clerk recognized them, and nearly fainted with surprise.

Hillary was awed to be living in the mansion where so many historic events had taken place. She thought of all the other First Ladies who had gone before her and pondered the roles they had played. The First Lady who impressed her most was Eleanor Roosevelt, wife of President Franklin D. Roosevelt. During the 1930s and 1940s, Eleanor was a passionate crusader for the poor. She was a powerful figure who helped to change the nation's social policy. Hillary looked

First Lady Eleanor Roosevelt promoting the March of Dimes to raise money for polio research

Hillary and Bill during a National Health Insurance speech in Ambridge, Pennsylvania

on Eleanor Roosevelt as a role model. She hoped that she could carry forward the work Eleanor began.

During the campaign, the Clintons promised to create a form of national health-care insurance. President Clinton appointed Hillary to head his National Health Care Task Force. She traveled the country, holding public hearings about health-care coverage. She invited leaders in the field to meet and plan a workable program. But the national health-care bill had many opponents. Insurers feared they

would be forced to cover people with costly chronic illnesses. Doctors worried that they would have to limit their fees. Even private citizens grew concerned that they would no longer be free to see the physician of their choice. In the end, Congress failed to pass the Clintons' health-care bill.

After the collapse of the health-care bill, Hillary did not retreat into the background. She continued to speak out on education, foster care, and other issues that concerned her. Critics argued that she was too active

in public affairs. The refrain was heard again and again, "We never voted for her!"

To make matters worse, reports surfaced that Bill and Hillary Clinton had been involved in unethical financial dealings in Arkansas. Records showed that Hillary earned astonishingly high returns on an investment. She denied having done anything illegal, but the rumors persisted. Furthermore, the Clintons were implicated in a questionable Arkansas land-development scheme. Hillary's

Hillary, Bill, and Chelsea singing Christmas carols at a White House tree-lighting ceremony

Confetti filled the United Center after Bill Clinton's presidential nomination at the close of the 1996 Democratic National Convention in Chicago.

alleged role in this "Whitewater affair" cast a shadow on her image.

Despite these problems, Bill Clinton was elected to a second presidential term in 1996. As she thought of the work that lay ahead of her, Hillary wondered how she could be most effective. She imagined herself in a conversation with Eleanor Roosevelt. She asked Eleanor what she should do. In her mind she could almost hear Eleanor reply, "Get out and do it, and don't make any excuses about it."

CHAPTER SEVEN

Looking Back, Looking Forward

☆ ☆ ☆ ☆ ☆ ☆ ☆ ☆ ☆ ☆ ☆ ☆ ☆ ☆ ☆

In 1996, Hillary Rodham Clinton wrote a book entitled *It Takes a Village*, which immediately became a best-seller. The book reflected her long-standing concern for children in the United States and around the world. The title came from an old African saying, "It takes a village to raise a child." Hillary's point was that the family alone cannot meet all of a child's needs. Children must also have good schools and safe streets. They need to be involved in religious and recreational activities. They have to know that opportunities await them when they complete their education.

In her book, Hillary paid a loving tribute to her

☆ ☆ ☆ ☆ ☆ ☆ ☆ ☆ ☆ ☆ ☆ ☆ ☆ ☆ ☆

Hillary visits a
kindergarten class-
room at the George
Washington
Nebbinger School in
Philadelphia where
Americorp volunteers
teach.

*Hillary holding her
book,* It Takes a
Village, *during a
book signing in a
suburban
Washington, D.C.,
bookstore*

Bill and Hillary at a ball to kick off the 1996 National Governors Association meeting at the White House

Chelsea and Hillary, wearing traditional Masai tribal necklaces, visit a Masai village in Tanzania, Africa, during their goodwill tour in the spring of 1997.

parents. She described how they encouraged her to have high aspirations, to be the best that she could possibly be. "My family, like every family I know of, was far from perfect," she wrote. "But however imperfect we were as individuals and as a unit, we were bound together by a sense of commitment and security. My mother and father did what parents do best— dedicated their time, energy, and money to their children, and made sacrifices to give us a better life."

First Lady, First Lawyer

✩ ✩

What did some other First Ladies do before moving to the White House? Hillary Clinton is the first presidential wife to have the same professional degree as her husband. (Although Lou Hoover did match Herbert's undergraduate degree in geology and later translated with him a mining text from Latin to English.) Hillary herself admitted that this had more to do with generational change than with her personally. Indeed, many early First Ladies were teachers since teaching was one of few careers open to respectable, middle-class women. Eleanor Roosevelt taught dance and later history. Grace Coolidge taught the hearing-impaired to speak. Caroline Harrison and Florence Harding were musicians and taught music. Ellen Wilson painted and exhibited her work. Jacqueline Kennedy worked as a photo-journalist, and Lady Bird Johnson ran a radio station. Pat Nixon taught high school. Betty Ford modeled and later became a fashion buyer for a department store.

Hillary and Chelsea watch a group of hippos in Ngorongoro Crater National Park, Tanzania.

As First Lady, Hillary Clinton found that she could not achieve all of her goals. She was buoyed through many disappointments by thoughts of her family, her church, and the community in which she grew up. "The pressures that knock you around all the time can undermine your sense of direction, your integrity as a person, and even who you are," she admitted in an interview. "In the world in which I'm living now, there is so much

Hillary and Chelsea at the Self-Employed Women's Association facility in Ahmadabad, India

In the fall of 1997, Bill and Hillary took Chelsea to Stanford University for her freshman year of college.

At one of Hillary Clinton's 50th birthday parties in Chicago, she was given a Chicago Cubs shirt.

The students at Field Elementary School in Park Ridge presented Hillary with a 50th birthday cake.

emphasis on the short-term and the secular. I feel really grateful to have some sense of faith and rooting that goes beyond that, and to be reminded that you have to try to stand for something bigger than yourself."

During her years in the White House, Hillary Clinton carried out the traditional duties of the First Lady. She supervised the redecorating of the Blue Room and the purchase of elegant new furniture. She was a gracious hostess at formal banquets and receptions. She was her husband's loyal partner and supporter. But Hillary was a new breed of First Lady, a woman who could stand firmly on her own. Her presence symbolized the changes that had swept the country since she gave her fiery commencement address at Wellesley. She still dreamed of creating something new in a world that no one quite understands.

✫ ✫ ✫ ✫ ✫ ✫ ✫ ✫ ✫ ✫ ✫ ✫ ✫ ✫ ✫

The Presidents and Their First Ladies

YEARS IN OFFICE			
President	*Birth–Death*	*First Lady*	*Birth–Death*
1789–1797			
George Washington	1732–1799	Martha Dandridge Custis Washington	1731–1802
1797–1801			
John Adams	1735–1826	Abigail Smith Adams	1744–1818
1801–1809			
Thomas Jefferson†	1743–1826		
1809–1817			
James Madison	1751–1836	Dolley Payne Todd Madison	1768–1849
1817–1825			
James Monroe	1758–1831	Elizabeth Kortright Monroe	1768–1830
1825–1829			
John Quincy Adams	1767–1848	Louisa Catherine Johnson Adams	1775–1852
1829–1837			
Andrew Jackson†	1767–1845		
1837–1841			
Martin Van Buren†	1782–1862		
1841			
William Henry Harrison‡	1773–1841		
1841–1845			
John Tyler	1790–1862	Letitia Christian Tyler (1841–1842)	1790–1842
		Julia Gardiner Tyler (1844–1845)	1820–1889
1845–1849			
James K. Polk	1795–1849	Sarah Childress Polk	1803–1891
1849–1850			
Zachary Taylor	1784–1850	Margaret Mackall Smith Taylor	1788–1852
1850–1853			
Millard Fillmore	1800–1874	Abigail Powers Fillmore	1798–1853
1853–1857			
Franklin Pierce	1804–1869	Jane Means Appleton Pierce	1806–1863
1857–1861			
James Buchanan*	1791–1868		
1861–1865			
Abraham Lincoln	1809–1865	Mary Todd Lincoln	1818–1882
1865–1869			
Andrew Johnson	1808–1875	Eliza McCardle Johnson	1810–1876
1869–1877			
Ulysses S. Grant	1822–1885	Julia Dent Grant	1826–1902
1877–1881			
Rutherford B. Hayes	1822–1893	Lucy Ware Webb Hayes	1831–1889
1881			
James A. Garfield	1831–1881	Lucretia Rudolph Garfield	1832–1918
1881–1885			
Chester A. Arthur†	1829–1886		

† wife died before he took office   ‡ wife too ill to accompany him to Washington   * never married

1885–1889			
Grover Cleveland	1837–1908	Frances Folsom Cleveland	1864–1947
1889–1893			
Benjamin Harrison	1833–1901	Caroline Lavinia Scott Harrison	1832–1892
1893–1897			
Grover Cleveland	1837–1908	Frances Folsom Cleveland	1864–1947
1897–1901			
William McKinley	1843–1901	Ida Saxton McKinley	1847–1907
1901–1909			
Theodore Roosevelt	1858–1919	Edith Kermit Carow Roosevelt	1861–1948
1909–1913			
William Howard Taft	1857–1930	Helen Herron Taft	1861–1943
1913–1921			
Woodrow Wilson	1856–1924	Ellen Louise Axson Wilson (1913–1914)	1860–1914
		Edith Bolling Galt Wilson (1915–1921)	1872–1961
1921–1923			
Warren G. Harding	1865–1923	Florence Kling Harding	1860–1924
1923–1929			
Calvin Coolidge	1872–1933	Grace Anna Goodhue Coolidge	1879–1957
1929–1933			
Herbert Hoover	1874–1964	Lou Henry Hoover	1874–1944
1933–1945			
Franklin D. Roosevelt	1882–1945	Anna Eleanor Roosevelt	1884–1962
1945–1953			
Harry S. Truman	1884–1972	Bess Wallace Truman	1885–1982
1953–1961			
Dwight D. Eisenhower	1890–1969	Mamie Geneva Doud Eisenhower	1896–1979
1961–1963			
John F. Kennedy	1917–1963	Jacqueline Bouvier Kennedy	1929–1994
1963–1969			
Lyndon B. Johnson	1908–1973	Claudia Taylor (Lady Bird) Johnson	1912–
1969–1974			
Richard Nixon	1913–1994	Patricia Ryan Nixon	1912–1993
1974–1977			
Gerald Ford	1913–	Elizabeth Bloomer Ford	1918–
1977–1981			
James Carter	1924–	Rosalynn Smith Carter	1927–
1981–1989			
Ronald Reagan	1911–	Nancy Davis Reagan	1923–
1989–1993			
George Bush	1924–	Barbara Pierce Bush	1925–
1993–			
William Jefferson Clinton	1946–	Hillary Rodham Clinton	1947–

Hillary Rodham Clinton Timeline

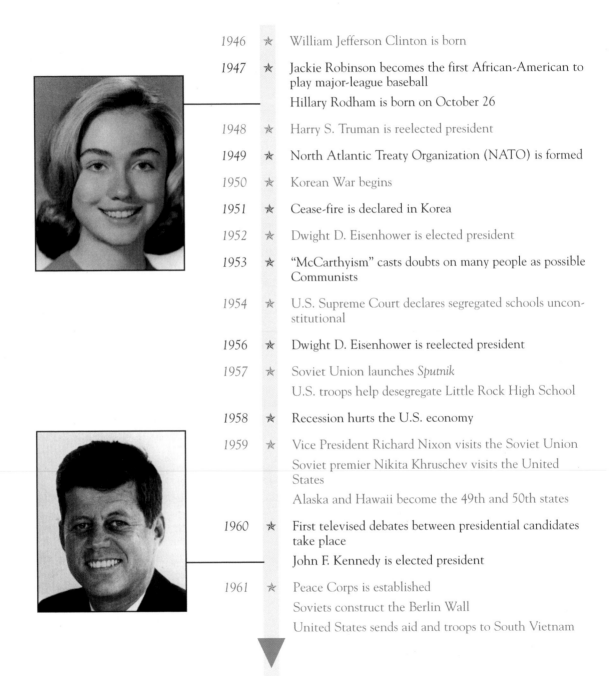

1946	★	William Jefferson Clinton is born
1947	★	Jackie Robinson becomes the first African-American to play major-league baseball
		Hillary Rodham is born on October 26
1948	★	Harry S. Truman is reelected president
1949	★	North Atlantic Treaty Organization (NATO) is formed
1950	★	Korean War begins
1951	★	Cease-fire is declared in Korea
1952	★	Dwight D. Eisenhower is elected president
1953	★	"McCarthyism" casts doubts on many people as possible Communists
1954	★	U.S. Supreme Court declares segregated schools unconstitutional
1956	★	Dwight D. Eisenhower is reelected president
1957	★	Soviet Union launches *Sputnik*
		U.S. troops help desegregate Little Rock High School
1958	★	Recession hurts the U.S. economy
1959	★	Vice President Richard Nixon visits the Soviet Union
		Soviet premier Nikita Khruschev visits the United States
		Alaska and Hawaii become the 49th and 50th states
1960	★	First televised debates between presidential candidates take place
		John F. Kennedy is elected president
1961	★	Peace Corps is established
		Soviets construct the Berlin Wall
		United States sends aid and troops to South Vietnam

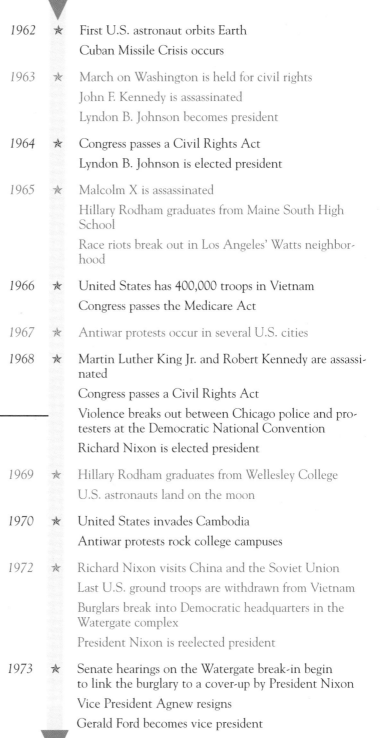

1962	★	First U.S. astronaut orbits Earth
		Cuban Missile Crisis occurs
1963	★	March on Washington is held for civil rights
		John F. Kennedy is assassinated
		Lyndon B. Johnson becomes president
1964	★	Congress passes a Civil Rights Act
		Lyndon B. Johnson is elected president
1965	★	Malcolm X is assassinated
		Hillary Rodham graduates from Maine South High School
		Race riots break out in Los Angeles' Watts neighborhood
1966	★	United States has 400,000 troops in Vietnam
		Congress passes the Medicare Act
1967	★	Antiwar protests occur in several U.S. cities
1968	★	Martin Luther King Jr. and Robert Kennedy are assassinated
		Congress passes a Civil Rights Act
		Violence breaks out between Chicago police and protesters at the Democratic National Convention
		Richard Nixon is elected president
1969	★	Hillary Rodham graduates from Wellesley College
		U.S. astronauts land on the moon
1970	★	United States invades Cambodia
		Antiwar protests rock college campuses
1972	★	Richard Nixon visits China and the Soviet Union
		Last U.S. ground troops are withdrawn from Vietnam
		Burglars break into Democratic headquarters in the Watergate complex
		President Nixon is reelected president
1973	★	Senate hearings on the Watergate break-in begin to link the burglary to a cover-up by President Nixon
		Vice President Agnew resigns
		Gerald Ford becomes vice president

1974	★	*Skylab* is launched
		Hillary Rodham helps the House Judiciary Committee assemble evidence to impeach President Nixon
		President Nixon resigns from office after the House Judiciary Committee sends articles of impeachment to the full House
		Gerald Ford becomes president, grants Nixon a pardon
1975	★	South Vietnam falls to the Communists
		Hillary Rodham marries Bill Clinton
1976	★	United States celebrates its bicentennial
		Bill Clinton is elected Arkansas state's attorney general
		Jimmy Carter is elected president
1977	★	President Carter pardons draft evaders from the Vietnam War period
		Hillary Rodham joins the Rose Law Firm
1978	★	Bill Clinton is elected governor of Arkansas
1979	★	Iranians capture the U.S. Embassy in Tehran, Iran, and hold U.S. citizens as hostages
1980	★	U.S. boycotts the summer Olympic Games in Moscow because the Soviet Union is at war in Afghanistan
		Hillary Rodham Clinton's only child, Chelsea, is born
		Bill Clinton is defeated for reelection as governor
		Ronald Reagan is elected president
1981	★	Iranians release the U.S. hostages
		President Reagan is shot but recovers
		Sandra Day O'Connor becomes the first woman appointed to the U.S. Supreme Court
1982	★	Amendment for equal rights for women fails to be ratified by enough states
		Bill Clinton is elected governor of Arkansas and is reelected every two years until 1992
1983	★	Sally Ride becomes the first U.S. woman astronaut
1984	★	President Reagan visits China
		First AIDS case in the United States is identified
		President Reagan is reelected

1986	★	Space shuttle *Challenger* explodes, killing all on board
1987	★	United States and Soviet Union sign nuclear missile reduction treaty
1988	★	George Bush is elected president
1989	★	Berlin Wall comes down Students hold demonstrations in China and the Chinese government cracks down on them
1990	★	Germany is reunited Iraq invades Kuwait
1991	★	U.S. leads a coalition of allies in Persian Gulf War Iraq is pushed from Kuwait Yugoslavia breaks up in civil war
1992	★	Ethnic cleansing begins in Yugoslavia Bill Clinton is elected president Israel and the Palestinians begin peace talks
1993	★	Congress passes the North American Free Trade Agreement (NAFTA)
1994	★	Bill and Hillary Clinton are plagued by the Whitewater scandal Republicans gain power in Congress U.S. peacekeeping forces land in Haiti
1995	★	U.S. terrorists bomb the federal building in Oklahoma City, killing 168 people Russian army battles rebels in Chechnya UN forces enter the war in Yugoslavia U.S. government shuts down because Congress and the president cannot agree on funding
1996	★	Hillary Clinton becomes the first First Lady to testify before a grand jury because of the Whitewater scandal Bill Clinton is reelected president
1997	★	President Clinton is plagued by scandals about his campaign fund-raising
1998	★	Iraq agrees to weapons' inspections by UN team after United States threatens new bombings.

Fast Facts about
Hillary Rodham Clinton

Born: October 26, 1947, in Chicago, Illinois

Parents: Hugh Rodham and Dorothy Howell Rodham

Education: Graduated with honors as a National Merit Scholarship finalist from Maine South High School, Park Ridge, Illinois (1965); graduated from Wellesley College (1969) and was the first student ever to address the graduating class; graduated from Yale University's Law School with honors (1973)

Careers: Researcher with the Yale Child Study Center; part of law team that assisted the House Judiciary Committee in bringing articles of impeachment against President Richard M. Nixon (1974); teacher at the University of Arkansas Fayetteville Law School (1974–1977); lawyer (1977–1979) and partner (1979–1993) with the Rose Law Firm in Little Rock

Marriage: To William Jefferson Clinton on October 11, 1975, in Fayetteville

Children: Chelsea Victoria Clinton, born on February 27, 1980, in Little Rock

Places She Lived: Chicago (1947–1950); Park Ridge, Illinois (1950–1969); Wellesley, Massachusetts (1965–1969); New Haven, Connecticut (1969–1973); Washington, D.C. (1973–1974, 1993–present); Fayetteville, Arkansas (1974–1976); Little Rock, Arkansas (1976–1993)

Major Achievements:

* Chaired the Educational Standards Committee as First Lady of Arkansas and brought about reforms for Arkansas schools (1983).

* Twice listed as one of the 100 most influential lawyers in the country.

* Headed the National Health Care Task Force and presented its findings and recommendations for a health-care bill to Congress (1993). Congress did not pass the Clintons' bill (1994).

* Wrote *It Takes a Village* (1995) and made an audio recording of it, which won the Grammy Award for best spoken-word performance (1996).

* Supervised the redecorating of the Blue Room in the White House.

* Took a leading role in planning and organizing William Jefferson Clinton's political campaigns (1974–1996).

Fast Facts about
William Jefferson Clinton's Presidency

Terms of Office: Elected in 1992 and 1996; served as the forty-second president of the United States from 1993 to the present

Vice President: Albert Gore from 1993 to the present

Major Policy Decisions and Legislation:

* Pushed a $496-billion deficit-reduction package through Congress (August 1993).
* Signed the Brady Bill, which made it harder for people to buy guns (November 1993).
* Supported passage of NAFTA (1993).
* Mediated peace accords between Israel and the Palestinians (1993).
* Sent U.S. peacekeeping forces to Haiti (1994).
* Sent U.S. peacekeeping forces to Bosnia (1995).
* Signed welfare reform bill that ended federal aid to many poor people (1996).
* Sent U.S. ships into the Persian Gulf and threatened Iraq with new bombings if Saddam Hussein did not allow the United Nations to check Iraq's chemical and nuclear weapon sites (1998).

Major Events:

* President Clinton appointed Janet Reno as the first woman U.S. attorney general (1993) and Madeleine Albright the first woman secretary of state (1997).
* President Clinton appointed Ruth Bader Ginsburg (1993) and Stephen Breyer (1994) as associate justices to the U.S. Supreme Court.
* For the first time in U.S. history, Congress told government workers not to report to work because Congress and the president could not agree on budgets for many departments (November 1995 and December 1995–January 1996).
* Two U.S. terrorists bombed the Murrah Federal Building in Oklahoma City, killing 168 people (April 1996).

Where to Visit

The Capitol Building
Constitution Avenue
Washington, D.C. 20510
(202) 225-3121

Museum of American History of the Smithsonian Institution
"First Ladies: Political and Public Image"
14th Street and Constitution Avenue NW
Washington, D.C.
(202) 357-2008

National Archives
Constitution Avenue
Washington, D.C.
(202) 501-5000

The National First Ladies Library
The Saxton McKinley House
331 S. Market Avenue
Canton, Ohio 44702

White House
1600 Pennsylvania Avenue
Washington, D.C. 20500
Visitor's Office: (202) 456-7041

White House Historical Association
740 Jackson Place NW
Washington, D.C. 20503
(202) 737-8292

Online Sites of Interest

Children's Defense Fund
http://www.childrensdefense.org.
Describes an organization that exists to provide a voice for children, who cannot vote, lobby, or speak for themselves; many links to organizations, networks, publications, and government agencies concerned with the welfare of children

The First Ladies of the United States of America
http://www2.whitehouse.gov/WH/glimpse/firstladies/html/firstladies.html
A portrait and biographical sketch of each First Lady plus links to other White House sites

History Happens
http://www.usahistory.com/presidents
A site that contains fast facts about William Jefferson Clinton

Internet Public Library, Presidents of the United States (IPL POTUS)
http://www.ipl.org/ref/POTUS/wjclinton.html
An excellent site with much information on Bill Clinton, including personal information and facts about his presidency; many links to other sites including biographies and other Internet resources

The National First Ladies Library
http://www.firstladies.org
The first virtual library devoted to the lives and legacies of America's First Ladies; includes a bibliography of books, articles, letters, and manuscripts by and about the nation's First Ladies; also includes a virtual tour, with pictures, of the restored Saxton McKinley House in Canton, Ohio, which houses the library

The White House
http://www.whitehouse.gov/WH/Welcome.html
Information about the current president and vice president; White House history and tours; biographies of past presidents and their families; a virtual tour of the historic building, current events, and much more

The White House for Kids
http://www.whitehouse.gov/WH/kids/html/kidshome.html
Socks the cat is your guide to this site, which includes information about White House kids, past and present; famous "First Pets," past and present; historic moments of the presidency; several issues of a newsletter called "Inside the White House,"and more

For Further Reading

Bach, Julie. *Hillary Rodham Clinton*. Edina, Minn.: Abdo & Daughters, 1993.

Devaney, John. *The Vietnam War*. New York: Franklin Watts, 1992.

Gormley, Beatrice. *First Ladies*. New York: Scholastic, Inc., 1997.

Gould, Lewis L. (ed.). *American First Ladies: Their Lives and Their Legacy*. New York: Garland Publishing, 1996.

Greenberg, Keith Elliot. *The Clintons, Bill & Hillary: Working Together in the White House*. Woodbridge, Conn.: 1994.

Guernsey, Joann Bren. *Hillary Rodham Clinton: A New Kind of First Lady*. The Achievers series. Minneapolis: Lerner Publications Company, 1993.

Jacobson, Doranne. *Presidents and First Ladies of the United States*. New York: Smithmark Publishers, Inc., 1995.

Kent, Zachary. *William Jefferson Clinton*. Encyclopedia of Presidents series. Chicago: Childrens Press, 1993.

Kilian, Pamela. *What Was Watergate? A Young Reader's Guide to Understanding an Era*. New York: St. Martin's Press, 1990.

Klapthor, Margaret Brown. *The First Ladies*. Washington, D.C.: White House Historical Association, 1994.

Kummer, Patricia K. *Arkansas*. One Nation series. Mankato, Minn.: Capstone Press, 1998.

Mayo, Edith P. (ed.). *The Smithsonian Book of the First Ladies: Their Lives, Times, and Issues*. New York: Henry Holt, 1996.

Milton, Joyce. *The Story of Hillary Rodham Clinton, First Lady of the United States*. New York: Yearling Books, 1994.

Sherrow, Victoria. *Hillary Rodham Clinton*. New York: Dillon Press, 1993.

Index

Page numbers in **boldface type** indicate illustrations

Photo Identifications

Cover: Portrait of First Lady Hillary Clinton
Page 8: Hillary Rodham, 1965 high-school yearbook photo
Page 22: Candid shot of Hillary Rodham (center), 1969 Wellesley College yearbook
Page 34: First-year law school student Hillary Rodham (right) at a League of Women Voters dinner
Page 48: Governor-elect Bill Clinton
Page 58: Bill, Hillary, and newborn Chelsea Clinton
Page 72: Governor Bill Clinton with Hillary and Chelsea announcing his bid for the Democratic presidential nomination
Page 88: Hillary Rodham Clinton at the 1997 National Medal of Arts ceremony

Photo Credits©

About the Author

Deborah Kent grew up in Little Falls, New Jersey, and received a B.A. in English from Oberlin College. She earned a master's degree from Smith College School of Social Work and worked for several years at the University Settlement House in New York City. For five years she lived in San Miguel de Allende, Mexico, where she wrote her first novel for young adults.

Ms. Kent is the author of a dozen young-adult novels as well as many titles in the Children's Press America the Beautiful series. *Hillary Rodham Clinton* is her second title in the Encyclopedia of First Ladies series. Other titles include *Jane Means Appleton Pierce*, *Eliza McCardle Johnson*, and *Elizabeth Kortright Monroe*.

Deborah Kent lives in Chicago with her husband, author R. Conrad Stein, and their daughter Janna.